"Mary, Jesus' wife"
A IV century Coptic Papyrus
True or false?

Georgeos Díaz-Montexano
Scientific Atlantology International Society (SAIS)

1

Coptic papyrus about "Mary, Jesus' wife"
Real or forgery?

By Georgeos Diaz-Montexano

Translation by César Guarde

This article was originally published online on September 18th in Facebook and Diaz's personal blog. The original Spanish version can be read here.

3

Coptic papyrus about
"Mary, Jesus' wife"

Real or forgery?

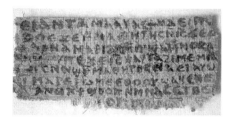

5

SUMMARY

7

Introductory note

Even if it is very difficult to date Coptic texts only through paleographic examination (the study of the style –or styles– of its writing), we still cannot speak of a text prior to the 4th century A.D.[1], at least three centuries after the mystery and passion of the Christ. This fact alone detracts greatly from its value as serious evidence, especially since this is the first and only specimen and it is impossible to establish a previous manuscript tradition or stemma to place the text in its historical context.

This being the case, this manuscript is insufficient to prove that its message has a well formed tradition behind, stretching back to the time Christ was alive. There is an absolute vacuum of three centuries without any proof of any single fragment of a similar text where Jesus –in first person– speaks about his wife or couple. There is also no evidence to relate this fragment to any of the Gospels or apocryphal writings from the first centuries of Christianity that we know.

In short, anything said about the marital status of Jesus Christ or His de facto partnership is only a matter of unfounded subjective speculation.

Paleography

The first striking feature we notice is the considerable difference in the state of conservation of the text between the recto (front) and verso (back) page. This is very unusual, almost unheard of. In the recto page (side 1) almost all characters are clearly readable, but not in the verso (side 2), where I can barely distinguish any letter, being unable to reconstruct any word. In my opinion, it can be said that this papyrus is "similar" to the prevailing style of the 4th and 5th centuries. And I say "similar" because in fact it does not fit exactly into one known style. However, when Dr. Karen L. King presented it to the media, she declared that the papyrus was consistent with the commonly used styles in the 4th century, maybe even older. Dr. King, who, I believe, is not an expert in papyrology and Coptic linguistics, consulted with two scholars: Roger

Bagnall, director of the Institute for the Study of the Ancient World in New York, and Annemarie Luijendijk, a papyrologist who worked in the edition of the Oxyrhyncus Papyri. The high-resolution images were provided by a Jewish scholar, Ariel Shisha-Halevy, professor of Linguistics at the Hebrew University of Jerusalem. Thus, the estimated date for the manuscript as presented by Dr. King, according to her, is based on the opinion or statements of these three scholars. However, I must say that I have never seen any other specimen with such an imprecise, grotesque, crude and careless style. I am sure it must be the work of an inept scribe without elegance or stylishness, for the text has no proportions between words, lines and even letters from a single word. Some characters are written with different styles, shapes, orientations and thickness. It looks as if it was the work of different hands randomly writing this or that letter or word. This is, in my opinion, absurd and unacceptable. An ancient scribe well versed in the Sahidic dialect of the Coptic language and its writing, even unskilled, could not be the author of this clumsy work.

11

Description

It is said the fragment measures 8x4 centimeters. The recto (side 1) consists of –at least– eight lines. The number of lines or letters in the verso (side 2) cannot be determined without further in situ analysis. No margins can be distinguished.

The text has no ornaments, neither ligogramms nor nexugramms. Letters present no inclination but their shapes and thickness are irregular at least. All letters are properly written following an imaginary "base" line but with little space between one line and the next. Thus, some letters are superimposed and there is no space for the auxiliary signs or diacritics of Coptic language that appear as lines above the entire syllables. Since there is no space between lines for this, it seems to me the scribe was not very familiar with the Coptic alphabet or the Uncial script.

Characters' size is inconsistent and their ink also varies considerably in intensity from one character to the other. This cannot be attributed to the deterioration, natural or not, of the specimen, but rather to a trembling and imprecise hand due to irregular pressure on the papyrus. Along these lines, it is important to point out how appropriate it is that the letters with the controversial expressions "my wife" (ⲧⲁ·ⲅⲓⲙⲉ), –4th line– and "I dwell with her" (ⲁⲛⲟⲕ ϯ·ϣⲟⲟⲡ ⲛⲙⲙⲁ.ⲥ) –7th line– Although misspelled as we will see later, and are the only ones that have been best preserved. It almost looks like as if the scribe was trying to highlight them by pressing his *kalamos*, so the reader will concentrate on those important words.

Rather than a kalamos, the thick borders seem to indicate a soft point of a brush. Thus, the writing seems "heavy" and unusual and the letters have no consistency at all. For example, the ei or epsilon (e), zēta (z), ou (omicron) and sima (sigma) are wide and round, like Greek uncials; but the alpha (alpha) is angular, me (m) is incorrectly written with two or four movements of brush, and ro (r) has a smaller head than usual; the u (ipsilon or y in Greek) has been written once with an underlined symbol and the shy (sh or š) appears with three different styles. The epsilon is clear example of these problems: sometimes it is slightly rising, sometimes from top to bottom, sometimes horizontally. Some of these differences can be found in a number of papyri, but never to such an extent. The scribe seems clearly unfamiliar with the Coptic alphabet. This is revealing, because the Coptic script used the Greek alphabet to transcribe Demonic texts and it is very similar to any Western writing system. If the forger was unfamiliar with them, it is possible that his native language was Arabic or Hebrew.

The characters

1. E **Є** (Ei) The ei is written in three different ways, with its horizontal strokes pointing up, down or parallels. This style changes even inside the same letter, and so does the thickness of the ink (Figure 1). The first ei is thick and dark but blurry and difficult to read. On the other side, the other three ei with a lack of ink, whether thick or not, are perfectly readable. They are closely written but the levels of ink differ and the orientation of the strokes changes from one letter to the next.

2. La **𝕸** (mei). The most prevalent shape of the letter *mei* in the papyrus does not appear before the 5th century (in coptic scripture). Usually, the central stroke between the vertical legs of the *mei* is slightly bended and sometimes it falls all the way down to the center of the right vertical stroke, with the left side thicker than the left side, It is almost always low, wider than high, and open up the sides at the bottom (**𝕸** and **𝕸** III-IV A.D. and **𝕸** s. IV A.D.), However, the *mei* in this papyrus looks more like a modern typography version (**M**), like modern font CS Coptic Manuscript. In really, the *mei* in this papyrus (**𝕸**, **𝕸** and **𝕸**) is similar to our Latin "M". We have some examples from the 4th century where the vertical strokes are parallel, but in such cases the central stroke forms an acute angle, like a "V" between two bars, whose angle drops to the base of the letter or even exceeds it frequently, what is not observed in any *mei* in this Papyrus, where almost seems more a Norwegian Rune or an archaic Greek sigma from Plato's times, but also remember the Greek uncial m (**M**).The scribe, thus, seems more

15

familiar with the modern typography of the Coptic alphabet, similar to our Latin "M" (Figure 2). Furthermore, the correct method for drawing the letter *mei* ( ) was a single, fluid stroke with the kalamos, but the *mei* in the papyrus has been outlined with two or four movements of the brush (it is even possible to notice how the different strokes superimpose themselves). But in this Papyrus see clear evidences that the author did in four movements, or in two times or phases, almost as if you draw two numbers one, but faced. First, from left to right, and then another stroke resembling a number one. Hence, shown clearly in several of the *mei* of this Papyrus the superposition of two strokes ꟿ (See details enlarged in Fig. 2). This way of writing the mei in the Coptic texts - so I know - it is not known, and if it is, certainly would a rarity, therefore, nothing unusual. But there are even more. I think that it is so unusual that it presents the mei written in four-stroke or two movements as a minimum in the word **ρωμε** (Línea 6) (line 6) with that strange shape almost of a Viking Rune, mainly due to the fact of having written this on top of a papyrus now

16

deformed and curved by the passage of time. It is possible this letter had to be written in this way because of the deformation of the papyrus. In Figure 3, we see how the middle section of the "V" stroke follows the concavity on the surface of the papyrus (Line 6). Since papyri were smoothen down for writing, the scribe should have used an already deteriorated specimen. The same can be seen in Line 5 with the previous *mei* of ΜΑΘΗΤΗC ("pupil"), where the letter follows the vertical fold making the "V" stroke slightly deformed. Other letters also seem affected by such irregularities in the surface of the specimen.

[Note of the translator: The author is suggesting that the text was written onto an older (maybe unused) papyrus. It is possible, then, that the text still visible in verso —six lines according to Dr. King, but she does not offer a translation in her recently rejected paper– is part of the older papyrus. This may explain its deterioration.]

3. Κ **Κ** (*kappa*). There is only one word that should contain a *kappa*: ΑΝΟΚ ("I") in Line 7. However, it looks more like ΑΝΩΧ. The *ou* **O** (*o*) seems to have been written like a long ō (ω,

Greek *omega*) and the final *kappa* **K** like a "X" (*kh*, Greek *xi*). **K** and X were interchangeable sometimes but not in their final position. Thus, the scribe is again at odds with the Coptic script.

4. *Tee* **†** (/*ti*/). This syllable appears twice in the recto page: In Line 1, we find **† naei**, "gave to me", and in Line 7, **†-ϣoon**, "give existence", "existing", hence **†naei †-ϣoon**, "I give existence" or "I am existing" [Note of the translator: This expression appears in Jn 8:58 and translate the Greek "egô eimi"]. But this *ti* is identical to the Greek cross, "+" - and in this papyrus- and not to the Coptic letter **†**, similar to a reversed "t" or Latin cross. As we see in styles of these same dates () in which is dated by the team of collaborators Dr. King. Although we can clearly see that they do not correspond.

5. *Y* **Y** (/*u*/, /*w*/). There are two different forms in the text. Lines 1, 4, and 5 present the usual *Y* () of the 4th century Coptic script. Line 7, however, presents an odd *Y* () similar to the Latin script, with a small stroke under the letter.

6. *Shy* ⲱ (*sh*). I see three different forms: Lines 5 , 6 and 7 . Line 5 seems, again, alien to the common Coptic script used in those times.

Other irregularities

7. A modern slash "/"? One week after my preliminary survey, first published in brief in my personal facebook (September 18ᵗʰ, 2012), and in my WordPress blog, the young but well-versed in Papyrology Alin Suciu published in his personal blog (09/26/2012) an interesting piece of information. Suciu points out to the presence of a symbol clearly similar to a modern slash "/", already noticed, as I later found out, by Dr. King. This symbol appears in Line 4, just before: ⲛⲉⲝⲉ ⲓⲥ ⲛⲁⲩ, "Jesus told them...". Suciu is right about his suspicions, but the reason I didn't include this issue in my paleographical survey was because, from my point of point, it looks more like damaged *kappa* (ⲕ). The reader can observe my reconstruction in Figure 3. In any case, a closer look without any contrast modification, as it can be seen clearly in the published high-resolution image, already shows that it is not just a simple "slash" symbol (oblique stroke). There are more visible elements allowing us to reconstruct it as a *kappa* (ⲕ); or

20

maybe another letter, but not just a "slash".
Therefore, from a paleographical point of view,
I don't consider it relevant to its authenticity.

8. Unknown "Pi" with a supralinear stroke.
What is rather interesting is what follows this
blurred *kappa* (κ): a *pi* (π) with an horizontal line
on top, a super-linear stroke also used as a
syllabic marker for the word *pedje*, "said", written
as follows: π̄εxε (Figura 4). I haven't found any
other similar case of an old specimen with a
stroke in that position. It is, without doubt, a
serious mistake inappropriate for an educated
native speaker able to make a copy of a Gospel.

**9. False mei redrawn over an unknown
letter.** The sixth sign in Line 2, after πεxε a
letter that Dr. King reads as mei with a super-
linear stroke, m, doesn't look like an original *mei*
but a clumsy attempt to cover a previous
undeleted sign (see Figure 5, with contrast
correction). I am unable to read the sign in the
substratum but, considering the intensity and
thickness of the horizontal stroke, it could not
have been a mei. Maybe it was a bad written n̄
(ēta) maybe blurred after attempting to draw a

mei. However, UV-colored spectrometry shows other signs under it.

10. A letter avoids a previous broken space. At the end of Line 2 I see a clear evidence to support the claim that the text was added to a previous papyrus fragment. The last letter *sêmma* **c** (s), has been adapted to the remaining space, making it artificially longer so it would look like its ends were lost when the papyrus was broken. That's why the sêmma looks like "crab claws", different from other normal items in the same papyrus (with one exception, v. infra).

11. A Greek beta converted into rô? Both Dr. King and the scholars who support her read **ⲁⲣⲛⲁ**, "deny", at the beginning of Line 3. However, a more detailed analysis of the image shows what I believe is neither a *rô* **ⲣ** (r) nor a *nê* **ⲛ** (n but blurred signs from the previous text in the papyrus. This rô looks like a previous *bêta* **ⲃ** (b) modified in order to write a *m* over it. Thus, it looks like a minor Greek *bêta*, **β** (Figura 6). If it was a nê, it would have been written over a different letter, which can be seen on the left, looking more like an êta **ⲏ** (h).

12. Modern punctuation marks. In the same line, between the second **ⲁ** in the alleged name of *Maria* and the beginning of **ⲙ̄ⲡϢⲁ**, there is another sign, impossible to read, that has been assumed to be a *mei* at the end of **ⲘⲀⲢⲒⲀⲘ**. But it does not look like a *mei* at all. There is another inconsistency: between the *pi* **ⲡ** (p) and the *šai* **ϣ** (sh), according to the experts' reading. At first sight, there is a sign similar to a horizontal stroke, like a small *iota* with a horizontal line at

the top and bottom, like a short Latin "I". This is unacceptable for a Coptic text, because **ⲙ̄ⲡϢⲁ** can never be broken into two parts, except in some modern editions where we can read **ⲙ̄ⲡ·Ϣⲁ**. This middle point is never used in manuscripts unless the scribe wants to divide a sentence. Thus, whether this sign represents a *dot*, an *slash* or an *hyphen*, it betrays, from my point of view, the hand of a forger who didn't know that these *dots* are only used in that position in modern editions of Coptic texts (post 2007), and never in ancient documents. The forgery, thus, must be recent.[iii]

23

13. Unknown rewritten letters. According to the experts, that word is followed by a *mei* with a super-linear stroke: ⲚⲘⲞⲤ. Not even with a high-resolution caption of that section can that letter be discerned. There are just two vertical bars, the left too wide and with a small oblique stroke to the left. There is no Coptic letter with that shape, and it resembles Nabataean or Ethiopian characters. I believe the damage around its center and the top right is intended, in order to hide a letter different from the *mei*. The other letters in this Line 3, *mei* Ⲙ, *ou* Ⲟ, *sēmma* Ⲥ and *alpha* ⲁ according to Dr. King's team, the last two *sēmma* and *alpha* cannot be properly identified with any Coptic letter. At best, a *zéta* Ⲍ or *hori* Ϩ was modified, combined with the previous *ou* with a horizontal stroke that crosses them, in order to look like a *sēmma*. The experts also assume what follows is an *alpha*, but the only Coptic letter that resembles its bad written strokes would be a *sēmma* or an *ou*. See Figure 7 for a comparison, using UV-colored spectrometry. This also shows that a brush, not a *kalamos*, seems to have been the instrument of the forgery.

24

14. Four rudely rewritten letters. Dr.King's team transcribes Line 5 as follows: ⲤⲚⲀⲰ̅ⲠⲘⲀⲐⲎⲦⲎⲤ ⲚⲀⲈⲒ, which translates as "She could be my disciple". This is questionable at most. The letters ⲧ, ⲏ, ⲥ and ⲛ show a different style, they are wider and darker, almost redrawn. There are other rather unusual elements, as reveled by high-resolution image analysis and UV-colored spectrometry. The *êta* (*h*) looks rather like a rounded Latin "A" with the horizontal stroke too high for an *êta*. The *sênma* looks rather like an squared *ei* totally alien to Coptic writing. It is too square and too different from other *sênmas* in the papyrus to be considered the same item. Finally, the *nê* seems to have been drawn over an previous rounded *sênma* or *êi*. The forger seems to have tried to modify the original letters from the papyrus so they would resemble the ⲘⲀⲐⲎⲦⲎⲤ ⲚⲀⲈⲒ. They are "by chance" just on top of the next relevant sentence, also darker (to attract attention) and redrawn: ⲦⲀⲈ̅ⲒⲘⲈ, "my woman/wife". This is almost grotesque. We also would like to point out that the UV-analysis reveals a modern brush (Figure 8).

25

15. Ink on the borders. Line 1, just above the letter Y (y) in ⲦⲀⲘⲀⲀⲨ, "my mother", some ink can be seen on the edge (Figure 9). If confirmed, this would prove that the papyrus was cut before writing the text on its surface. The forger tried to write a Y very close to the edge, like a broken letter with some missing strokes. The reader would believe this was actually cut after writing on its surface. However, some ink dripped off the edge. If the papyrus was authentic, the edge should be clear of any trace of ink.

16. A symbol from the original papyrus? The bottom left shows some kind of very small and unidentified decorative symbol or drawing (Figure 10). It could be a symbol from a magical papyrus and, if so, it should be authenticated by an expert in this field. This could shed some light on the original papyrus.

17. Hairs adhered. According to Dr. King, she received the papyrus already inside the protective glass. The images on the Internet are, thus, pictures of the papyrus inside its protective glass. However, I have found traces of what could be human hairs near the top left edge, just

26

above the **ⲁ** after **ⲧ** in **ⲦⲀⲘⲀⲀⲨ**, "my mother" (Line 11). Three wavy (maybe because of continuous dyeing), long, grey, brown dyed hairs can be seen (Figure 11-a). I believe they are from a white woman in her 50's, maybe older. The hair looks too long for a common Western man, but it could be from a Middle East male. However, since it seems dyed, that's very unlikely. If this is the case, the hairs should be analyzed in order to verify the integrity of the papyrus.

18. An *alpha* written after the papyrus got damaged or distorted. The *alpha* just under the human hairs seems to have been written with a brush over an already distorted old surface, a long vertical crease (Figure 11-b). It is easy to see that the thickest stroke happens to be just in these two folds. This could only happen if the wet ink was added over an old deformed surface.

27

Ethnic cultural identification of the forger

From the very beginning I observed that the strokes seem to be "ad sinistrorsum", like most Arabs and Jewish. Because the writing was made with a brush, not a *kalamos*, I could not be totally sure about this. I asked for help to a visual artist and art restoration expert, the Argentinean Virginia Laurentti. I sent her high-resolution images with enhanced details where I could see traces of brush and, after some hours, she confirmed my survey about the direction of the writing: the horizontal strokes were drawn from right to left and the vertical ones from bottom to top. The circular shapes where drawn from bottom to top and clockwise. Mrs. Laurentti also declared that some kind of paper (or maybe an sponge) was used to absorb the excess of ink just after writing every word. That may have been the reason some letters are less blurred. In the picture these traces are clearly visible. As she states:

"It can be seen, from the size of the papyrus and the shape in the edges of the letters that the writer used a round brush with smooth bristles (probably number 1),

rather than a brush with harder or shorter bristles different from those I mentioned. The weare follows from bottom to top, and it looks like most of the weight (ink) happens to be dissolved upwards. The third image you showed me (Figure 8), the letter shaped like an "N" seems to have been overwritten. The ink (in all the letters from Figure 7) looks like an spattering. There is an excess of ink in the brush (I should say this can help you to determine how skillful the scribe was, and to compare it with any old writing). This kind of analysis is usually used to study the painters' technique. It is also possible that the scribe has used something (i.e., paper) over the papyrus to simulate the wearing out of the ink and remove it when added in excess; also the letter C (sèmma) in the second image (Figure 8), seems to follow this dispersion pattern. The M (also in the second image) shows some "wrinkles", like there was something pushing, maybe a trace of some absorbent paper. I t could use some simple essays to show it to you. What I pointed out in the picture (Figure 12) is the result of pressure; the marks and the dispersion of the ink are visible. About what I previously said about the author writing (vertical and oblique strokes) from bottom to top, a simple experiment with a brush and wash drawing would be enough: most of the ink is exposed when the brush touched the surface for the first time and then most letters have more ink in the bottom and right sides. This is clear in the first image of the second set you sent me (Figure 13). It is clearly a brush! Horizontal strokes are drawn

29

*from right to left and from bottom to top, mostly.
Sometimes the contrary seems true (Figure 14). The O
begin like a semicircle; some of them, not all, seem to have
been written from bottom to top. They end with another
semicircle, also from bottom to top. The C (sêmma) is
outlined likewise".*

With these words does Virginia Laurentti, an art
restoration expert, confirms my initial survey.
Hence, we can assume the author of this text
wrote circular shapes clockwise. Vertical and
oblique strokes were "ad sinistrorsum", from
right to left, like the writing in Islamic and
Jewish countries. It is possible that this papyrus
came from Egypt, where the black market of
antiquities is part of the idiosyncrasy of the
country and the most common language is the
Egyptian Arabic, written using the Arabic alifbāt
(abyad), from right to left. Islamic writers do
actually write circular letters clockwise and from
bottom to top; horizontal strokes are also from
right to left. If the forger was from an Islamic
country, that could explain his/her unfamiliarity
with the Coptic language and script, closer to
Western Greek or Latin characters. Ancient
Coptic was never written from right to left and
letters were drawn neither clockwise nor from
bottom to top. Hence, I believe the forger was

30

not well-versed in Coptic writing and his mother language was probably written clockwise. He/she was probably an Arab or Muslim from Egypt.

Translation:

Obverse or recto (Side 1)

1 ....] no [to] me. My mother gave me li[fe? ....

2 ....] the disciples told Jesus [....

3 ....] deny her/it Mary worth of it [is not?] ....

4 ....] said Jesus to them: "My woman [....

5 ....] she could be my disciple [....

6 ....] The man .... in the Desert [....

7 ....] I give existence with her because [....

8 ....] a [....

Reverse (Side 2)

(... Unreadable characters with little traces of ink ...).

Notes

Line 3: ⲘⲀⲢⲒⲀⲘ ⲘⲡϢⲀ ⲘⲘⲟ·ⲥ. Here ⲘⲡϢⲀ, "to be worth", is a transitive verb with a 3rd person feminine object ⲘⲘⲟ·ⲥ: "Mary is worthy of her/it...". Dr. King translates "Mary is worthy of it". Moreover, it could be a bad building of ⲘⲘⲟ·ⲥ, which translates as, "(she) is not." It would therefore be: literally: "Mary is worthy (or not)", although I still sounds absurd, roughly translates to: "Mary is not worthy." Another mistake? This could be another irregularity from an inept scribe, so is the possible negation at the end of the sentence.

Line 4. Undoubtely the most controversial. Media has published the reading "my wife", but in Classical Sahidic Coptic "my woman/my wife" would be ⲦⲀ·ⲤϩⲒⲘⲉ. Here we have ⲦⲀ·ϩⲒⲘⲉ, without ⲥ (s), is a rare form. Not necessarily "my wife". It could be a "non-legal" relationship, that is to say, some sort of companion, girlfriend or lover who lives with him. But it doesn't stop here: ⲦⲀ·ϩⲒⲘⲉ, in the same Sahidic dialect, could be understood as "my ticket", "my load" or "my price" ("what I should pay")[10]. This word is documented to have been used in relation to "fare" or "ticket", the amount of money that should be paid for a ship journey and also for the ship's load. It is possible that an Gnostic text would have used this word with a metaphorical or symbolic meaning. The whole sequence follows: ⲡⲉⲝⲉ ⲓ̅ⲥ̅ ⲛⲁ·ⲩ ⲧⲁ·ϩⲓⲙⲉ. According to Dr. King's team of experts, it translates as "Jesus said to them: "My wife…". But it could also be rendered as "Jesus said to them: "My ticket/load/fare (to pay)". If the text was authentic, Jesus could continue talking about the "price" he would have to pay or the "load" he had to endure, etc. But there is something very wrong with this sequence, something that show, in my opinion, that this text is a forgery: the omission of ⲝⲉ, introducing direct speech, and which must be (compulsorily) placed before ⲧⲁ·ϩⲓⲙⲉ, "my wife" or "my ticket/price/load". Thus, the sequence should be: ⲡⲉⲝⲉ ⲓ̅ⲥ̅ ⲛⲁ·ⲩ ⲝⲉ ⲧⲁ·ϩⲓⲙⲉ. This is basic knowledge of Sahidic Coptic dialect, the one used in this papyrus, which is supposedly to

33

have been written by a native speaker of Coptic in the 4th century A.D.

Line 6: ϢⲀϤⲉ translates as "desert", but it could be a variant of ϢⲀϤⲓ, "swollen". Without an antecedent it is difficult to translate. It could be "the man (or people) in the desert (of) ..." or "the man (or the people) ... swollen," maybe a reference to evil people.

Line 7: The media has reported, following Dr. King, that this line reads "I dwell with her", that is to say, Jesus was living *de facto* with Maria. I would like to question this reading: ⲀⲚⲞⲔ Ⲧ.ϢⲞⲞⲠ ⲚⲘⲘⲀ.Ⲥ ⲈⲦⲂⲈ, "I give existence with her ("the "Being" or "the happening"")". ¿Why...", rather than "I [Jesus] dwell with her [Maria]...", according Dr. King. ϢⲞⲞⲠ —as qualitative of ϢⲰⲠⲈ- means here "to come into existence", and it cannot be interpreted as "living" or "dwelling place". If the author of this document really intended to write what Dr. King said, "... I live (or I am) with her ..." then wrote it all in a way absurd and farfetched. I do not think that a former clerk versed (birth insurance) in

34

the Sahidic dialect of the Coptic language could
write something similar.

Conclusion:

Therefore, I do not consider this specimen contains a fragment of a longer Coptic text written in Sahidic dialect by a competent scribe or, as Dr. King calls it, "The Gospel of Jesus's Wife". Many are the inconsistencies, many the problems which beset us. From our partial analysis it is clearly a forgery that cannot be in any way dated back to early Christianity. Likewise, the forger ignores the basic principles of Coptic writing and grammar.

[Note of the translator: It seems important to me the fact that it is Dr. King, a well-known scholar who has a great interest in the relation and position of women in early Christianity, the one who has receive the papyrus. I am not suggesting Dr. King has anything to do with the forgery, but the perpetrators obviously knew who the best "receptacle" for the debate was. Sure a fragment of an unknown text with just the words "Jesus" and "wife" and "dwell with me" preserved being sold to "an authority on women's roles in the early church" should be suspicious to everyone!].

36

In this papyrus, the forger has tried to imitate a vulgar or common style usually used in personal letters, commercial contracts or magical papyri, but the number of errors, omissions —maybe to purposely single it out—. However, his "singled out" style is absurd. Even if they would make sense in a personal or commercial document, they are totally out of place in a religious text or, following Dr. King's team statements, an unknown Gospel. I do not believe it was a matter of chance that the forger chose Dr. King. She is not a papyrologist or an expert in Coptic language. However, her personal CV shows a personal and academic dedication to vindicate the position of women in early Christianity and its significant role in the transmission of Christian faith, specially of Mary Magdalene, the so-called "wife of Jesus". Dr. King would have receive this papyrus very enthusiastically as new evidence for her ideological and religious beliefs. Moreover, I believe modern editions of Apocryphal Gospels have been used to incorporate —per grandis ignorantia— punctuation and separation marks alien to ancient papyri.

37

FIGURAS

Figura 1. Figure 1. Four completely different types of E Coptic in style, orientation and thickness of it. Different orientations and thickness: (1) inked bold and better than those around her, yet inaccurate or illegible. (2) broad strokes but almost out of ink and upward orientation. (3) thick and thin strokes while facing up on the top bar and extremely up-acute-angled at the bottom, while the core remains almost horizontally, but only outgoing. I know of no example of this unusual style of writing an E Coptic. (4) Rough half round thick, slightly curved, corresponding to a classic style uncial quite completely the difference remaining as if it were the other hand.

Figura 2. The first two photos are examples of texts to III-IV century AD The predominant form of *mei* used here does not correspond to

39

any of the Coptic or Greek styles known of the early centuries (before V century AD), where it presents clear curvature in the transom or central bar connecting the two vertical bars or right angle falls to the base thereof and below even, and is almost always lower and wider than high open sideways in the lower ends (ⲙ and ⲙ centuries III-IV A.D. and ⲙ IV A.D.), but mei this papyrus is shaped mei suspiciously similar to the fonts Coptic certain modern (ⲙ), as in the source known as CS Coptic Manuscript.

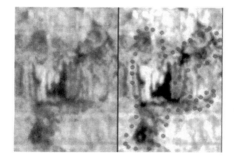

Figura 3.

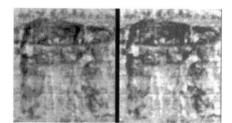

Figura 4.

41

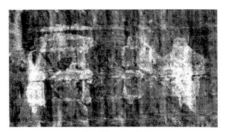

Figura 5.

Figura 6.

43

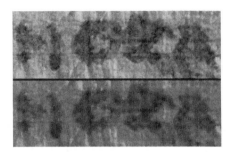

Figura 7.

Figura 8.

44

Figura 9.

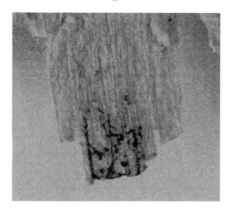

Figura 10.

45

Figura 11.

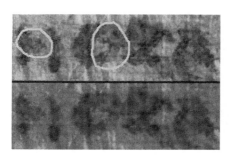

Figura 12.

Figura 13.

47

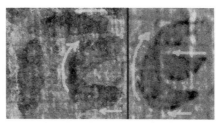

Figura 14. Examples of sinistrorsos strokes and from bottom to top. Left on i̅c̅ "Jesús" (Line 4). On the right, last and Line 2.

Professor Karen L. King, in her office at Harvard Divinity School, held a fragment of papyrus that she says was written in Coptic in the fourth century and contains a reference to Jesus' wife.

http://www.hds.harvard.edu/people/faculty/karen-l-king

Recursos:

http://www.schoyencollection.com/bibleCoptic.html
http://library.duke.edu/rubenstein/scriptorium/papyrus
/images/150dpi/797v-at150.gif
http://library.duke.edu/rubenstein/scriptorium/papyrus
/images/150dpi/258r-at150.gif
http://library.duke.edu/rubenstein/scriptorium/papyrus
/images/150dpi/475-at150.gif

http://www.hds.harvard.edu/faculty-research/research-
projects/the-gospel-of-jesuss-wife
http://www.nytimes.com/2012/09/19/us/historian-
says-piece-of-papyrus-refers-to-jesus-wife.html?_r=0

Biblia Coptica; F.-J. Schmitz and G. Mink (eds.),
Liste der koptischen Handschriften des Neuen
Testaments, 1: Die sahidischen Handschriften
der Evangelien (ANTF 8), Berlin and New
York, 1986; 2.1 (ANTF 13), Berlin and New
York, 1989; 2.2 (ANTF 15), Berlin and New
York, 1991.

Horner, Northern Dialect; Horner, Southern
Dialect. 6.1.4.3.

L.T. Lefort and M. Wilmet, Concordance du
Nouveau Testament sahidique, vol. I: Les mots
d'origine grecque (CSCO 124), Louvain, 1950

(Lefort); vol. II: Les mots Autochtones, 1
(CSCO 173), 1957; 2 (CSCO 183), 1958; 3
(CSCO 185), 1959 (Wilmet).

Brankaer, Johanna, Coptic: A Learning
Grammar (Sahidic), Otto Harrassowitz Verlag,
2010, ISBN: 3447058943, 9783447058940.

---

[1] 'Aerae Domini', that is, "Of the Age of the Lord." Not
'Anno Domini', "In the Year of the Lord", which would
be wrong.

[2] Alin Suciu, a papyrologist University of Hamburg,
was the first (September 19, 2012), after my first report
preliminary paleographic September 18, 2012, in-state
with conviction-that was false. Two days later, Francis
Watson of Durham University (September 21, 2012)
supported this hypothesis and publicly argued that it
was a falsification made in modern times. Unlike my
paleographical and grammatical arguments, have
focused their origin in the textual composition. Dr.
Watson I have made it clear that this falsification has
been conducted mainly by fragments taken from an
apocryphal: The Gospel of Thomas. Other scholars
subsequently joined his arguments, also centered at the
origin of the composition of the texts. But so far, I have
only published a report paleographic (albeit preliminary)
very detailed, almost letter by letter, proving the

falsification of this document, mainly from paleography and to a lesser extent from the grammar.

[3] See, for example, the grammar of Sahidic by John Martin Plumley, in the edition of 2007, Introduction to Sahidic Coptic. With Exercises & Vocabularies, by Laytony Bentley, 2007, and "Coptic: A Learning Grammar (Sahidic)," by Johanna Brankaer, 2010.

[4] See example:
http://library.duke.edu/rubenstein/scriptorium/papyrus/images/150dpi/475-at150.gif

[5] ⲓ̅ⲥ̅ are abbreviation of ⲓ̅ⲉ̅ⲥ̅ⲟ̅ⲩ̅ⲥ̅, Jesus.

[6] Sahidic form of ϩⲎⲘⲈ (Crum. 675b).

Made in the USA
San Bernardino, CA
14 October 2016